Pumpkin
The Puppy Who Saved Halloween!

8.5 x 8.5"

76 pages

Once upon a time..... on a moonlit Halloween night.... in the cheerful town of Spookville... a high-spirited puppy named Pumpkin frolicked through the streets. His fluffy tail twitching with anticipation.

Pumpkin was not an ordinary pup. He had a bountiful heart with the desire to spread joy and love to those less fortunate.

Spookville was ready for Halloween.
With Jack-o-lanterns grinning,
cobwebs draped over doorways
and shadows
dancing
in the candlelight.

The air was filled with the
sweet scent of candy
and the laughter of children
in the distance.

As Pumpkin scurried along
on this Halloween night,
he noticed a group of puppies gathered
together.

He detected a sense
of sadness in their eyes.
They did not have
any Halloween
treats.

This bothered Pumpkin. He decided that no pup should be without treats on this special night.

Pumpkin was determined to find Halloween goodies for his new friends. He sniffed out smells of treats along with the sounds of laughter and joy.

Spookville's streets were filled
with children busily
dressed as ghosts
and goblins.

Pumpkin was determined to help his newfound friends. He continued to wander through Spookville, looking for Halloween treats.

Pumpkin at long last came upon a friendly witch named Glendora. When Pumpkin told her his dilemma. Glendora was not ready to help!

Glendora asked: why should I help?

Pumpkin responded: because you can!

It is important to remember

to always help others. if you can.

Pumpkin woofed and wagged his tail so hard he convinced Glendora to open her heart and share her Halloween treats with Pumpkin's newfound friends.

With treats in his mouth,
Pumpkin bolted back to his
friends with Halloween candy
to share with his newfound
friends.

When the puppies saw Pumpkin,
they became excited. They were
so hungry and tired.

Pumpkin had brought back biskets, chewy bones, and some spooky-shaped toys!

Pumpkin loved Halloween because it was a time to share warmth, kindness, and love with others.

He wanted the puppies to know that Halloween is not only about candy and costumes.

The homeless puppies once distraught. now expressed their gratitude to Pumpkin.

Together the furry friends enjoyed their treats underneath the glow of the Halloween moon.

Pumpkin's generous heart had transformed this night into a memorable moment.

....and so, under the enchanting Halloween moon

The spirit of generosity spread like wildfire!

proving that even a small act of kindness

can light up the darkest corner and bring joy to those in need.

.... and so... on this Halloween night, the cozy town of Spookville witnessed the magic of a puppy named Pumpkin.

bring kindness, joy, and love to others

....on this Halloween night!

The moral of this story is that tiny acts of kindness make a huge difference in the lives of others who are less fortunate!

Pumpkin's actions remind us that kindness and generosity bring joy to others.

Did you enjoy this story?
We would love to hear from you.
Please complete a review
on Amazon.
Positive feedback is
always appreciated.
Thank you!

A letter from Pumpkin to you!

Hi,

It is nice to meet you. I am Pumpkin the puppy who helped my new friends to find treats on Halloween. I will be sharing more of my adventures with you. I hope to see you again, soon!

Thank you,

Woof Woof!

10594034R00044